Hildegard of Bingen

by
Angelo Cardinal Amato

All booklets are published thanks to the generous support of the members of the Catholic Truth Society

CATHOLIC TRUTH SOCIETY
PUBLISHERS TO THE HOLY SEE

Contents

The 'Canonisation Equivalent'. 3

Biographical Sketch 7

Attempts at Canonisation. 12

Exemplarity of Life 16

The Reputation of Holiness and Miracles 23

Eminens Doctrina 25

The Perennial Validity of Hildegard 36

Message of Holiness 44

Benedict XVI and Hildegard of Bingen. 45

All rights reserved. This edition first published 2013 by The Incorporated Catholic Truth Society, 40-46 Harleyford Road London SE11 5AY Tel: 020 7640 0042 Fax: 020 7640 0046. Copyright © 2012 Libreria Editrice Vaticana. Translated by Matthew Sherry. © 2013 The Incorporated Catholic Truth Society in this English language edition.

ISBN 978 1 86082 885 0

The 'Canonisation Equivalent'

On 10th May 2012, the Holy Father Benedict XVI "extended to the Universal Church the liturgical devotion in honour of St Hildegard of Bingen, a professed nun of the Order of St Benedict, who was born in Bermersheim (Germany) in 1098 and died in Rupertsberg (Germany) on 17th September 1179, inscribing her in the catalogue of the saints." This is the brief statement that appeared in *L'Osservatore Romano* on 11th May 2012.

So we ask ourselves: wasn't Hildegard of Bingen already considered a saint before this? Blessed John Paul II, in 1979, had said of her: "A light of her people and of her time, St Hildegard of Bingen shines more brightly during these days in which we celebrate the eight hundredth anniversary of her departure from this world, the malice and sin of which she kept far away from her, but who, driven by the love of Christ, benefitted by countless gifts to live in eternity with God."[1] And Benedict XVI dedicated two catecheses to her in September 2010, affirming: "Various female figures stand out for the holiness of their lives and the wealth of their teaching even in those centuries of history that we usually call the Middle Ages. Today I would like to begin to present one of them to you: St Hildegard of Bingen, who lived in Germany in the twelfth century."[2]

And so: who was Hildegard of Bingen, and why this delayed official recognition of her sanctity?

An unusual case for sainthood

Let us say at the beginning that the case of 'St' Hildegard of Bingen is very unusual for at least two reasons. The first concerns the particular historical moment (which spans from 1170/71 to 1234), in which there had not yet been a definitive transition from canonisation by the bishop to canonisation by the Pope. As a result, the first steps for canonisation, taken immediately after the death of the Rhenish abbess in 1179, have the feel of a climate of transition, in which the canonical procedures to be followed in this regard were not yet well defined.

The second reason is represented by the deeply rooted and widely shared conviction of the holiness of Hildegard of Bingen, which dates back to the period immediately following her death, between the end of the twelfth century and in the first decades of the thirteenth century, a conviction that, in any case, continued practically uninterrupted down to our time and makes reference to a *de facto* canonisation of the Rhenish mystic, although she had never been proclaimed a saint *de iure*.

The biographical sources, both at the time of her death and later, clearly speak of her as 'saint' or 'blessed.'

The reputation of holiness was further reinforced by the veneration reserved for her tomb and her relics, and also by the liturgical devotion bestowed upon her with the approval of the ecclesiastical authorities, not only in Mainz, but afterward also in Trier, Speyer, Limburg and in the whole Benedictine order.

After this, and down to our own time, her name has been found in both the local and the official martyrologies of the Roman Church, always accompanied by the title of 'Saint.' Moreover, in addition to the three popes who had the clear intention of proceeding with the canonisation of Hildegard of Bingen - Gregory IX, Innocence IV and John XXII - there have also been supreme pontiffs who have designated her with the title of 'Saint,' including Clement XIII, Pius XII and - as we have already seen - John Paul II and Benedict XVI. This common and generalised conviction led to the implicit belief that a specific procedure for Hildegard of Bingen, already seen as canonised, was unnecessary or superfluous.

In any case, in order to regularise the situation, Benedict XVI, taking note of the existence since time immemorial of a solid and constant *fama sanctitatis et miraculorum*, proceeded with the canonisation equivalent according to the legislation of Urban VIII (1623-1644), afterward theorised definitively by Prospero Lambertini, who later became Pope Benedict XIV (1740-1758).[3] In the canonisation equivalent:

"the Supreme Pontiff commands that a servant of God - who is found to be in ancient possession of devotion and about whose heroic virtues or martyrdom and miracles there is a constant and common declaration on the part of trustworthy historians, and has uninterrupted fame as a wonder-worker - should be honoured in the Universal Church with the recitation of the office and the celebration of the Mass on some particular day, without any definitive formal sentence, without any juridical process whatsoever beforehand, without having carried out the usual ceremonies."[4]

The canonisation equivalent of Hildegard of Bingen - *nulla accedente formali sententia definitiva, nullis praemissis iudicialibus processibus, nullisque consuetis caeremoniis adhibitis* - took place at the decision of Pope Benedict XVI on 10th May 2012. The measure was taken following numerous requests from pastors and faithful who wanted to see the Rhenish abbess officially canonised.

This is not a rare case. Examples of 'canonisation equivalents' are listed by Prospero Lambertini in chapter XLI of Book I of his *magnum opus*. He cites the cases of Saints Romuald, Norbert, Bruno, Peter Nolasco, Raymond Nonnatus, Giovanni Maria de Matha, Felix of Valois, Margaret of Scotland, Stephen of Hungary, Wenceslaus of Bohemia, Gregory VII and Gertrude the Great.

Biographical Sketch

Hildegard of Bingen was born in 1098 in Bermersheim to a family of rich and noble landowners. At the age of eight she was accepted as an '*oblate*' in the women's monastery adjoining the Benedictine abbey of Disibodenberg, where she was educated by Jutta of Sponheim and where she took the veil around 1115, making her religious profession at the hands of Bishop Otto of Bamberg.

At the death of Jutta, around the year 1136, the 38-year-old Hildegard was called to succeed her as '*magistra*,' basing her spirituality on the Benedictine tradition of spiritual balance and ascetic moderation. Around 1140 her mystical experiences and visions intensified, as described and interpreted later with the help of the monk Volmar in *Scivias* and in some of her other writings. In her initial uncertainty about the origin and value of her experiences and visions she turned in search of advice, around 1156, to Bernard of Clairvaux, from whom she received complete approval. Between November 1147 and February 1148, through Bishop Henry of Mainz and Abbot Kuno of Disibodenberg, Hildegard also consulted Pope Eugene III, who was at Trier at the time, from whom she received what amounted to papal confirmation of her visions and writings.

Following an increase in the number of nuns, due above all to the great esteem in which she was held, and with the emergence of conflict with the neighbouring Benedictine monks of Disibodenberg, around the year 1150 she was able to found, using her family's assets and financial support from the wealthy von Stade family, a monastery of her own on the Rupertsberg, at the confluence of the Nahe and the Rhine, in the environs of Bingen, where she moved together with twenty nuns, all of noble birth.

In 1165, both because of the great number of requests for admission and above all in order to permit non-noble candidates to enter the Benedictine monastic life, Hildegard founded a new monastery in Eibingen, on the opposite bank of the Rhine, renovating an old building belonging to the Augustinians and appointing a prioress for day-to-day administration. She remained the sole abbess of both monasteries, Rupertsburg and Eibingen: although she normally resided at Rupertsberg, she went twice weekly by boat to the monastery of Eibingen to guarantee the two foundations a unity of spiritual orientation, administrative direction and governance.

Within the cloister walls she took great care of the spiritual and material life of the community, with special emphasis on the fraternal spirit, cultural education and the liturgy, often enlivened by songs of her own composition, and treating the illnesses of her fellow sisters with herbs that she herself cultivated and prepared. She gave the community a very balanced spiritual life, avoiding extremes of asceticism that were not rare at the time and distributing with moderation the times of fasting, silence and prayer, which she balanced with times of work, rest and wholesome recreation. In the outside world she made active efforts to reinvigorate the Christian spirit and to strengthen religious practice, seeking also to combat the heretical tendencies of the Cathars and to promote the reform of the Church, and above all to improve the discipline and way of life of the clergy.

At the invitation first of Adrian IV (1154-1159) and then of Alexander III (1159-1181), the abbess of Rupertsberg and Eibingen exercised a fruitful apostolate - unusual for a woman at the time, and even more so for a nun officially kept in cloister - making from 1159 to perhaps 1171 three or probably four great apostolic voyages, and preaching even in the public squares and in various cathedral churches, including in Cologne, Trier, Liège, Mainz, Metz, Werden, Bamberg and Würzburg.

With regard to reform in particular, she was not afraid to urge eminent members of the ecclesiastical hierarchy and numerous representatives of the clergy to more consistent Christian conduct. She also addressed very harsh words to Emperor Frederick I (1122-1190), to whom she was bound by sentiments of friendship, but who had dared to appoint and oppose to Alexander III (1159-1181), the legitimate pope, the three antipopes Victor IV (1159-1164), Paschal III (1164-1168) and Callistus III (1179-1180).

A gifted expert in many areas

In her numerous and well-known works, Hildegard of Bingen not only describes her visions and mystical experiences, but also demonstrates her knowledge as a musician, cosmologist, artist, dramaturge, naturalist, healer, philosopher and composer.

Among her most famous works, apart from her voluminous correspondence, mention must be made of *Scivias sive Visionum ac Revelationum Libri Tres*, perhaps her best-known composition, containing the contents of twenty-six visions; the *Liber Divinorum Operum*; the *Liber Vitae Meritorum*, and other lesser writings of various genres and lengths.

She was often written to or visited at the Benedictine monastery on the Rupertsberg by eminent figures or ordinary people who turned to the Rhenish abbess with trust and in search of exhortation, advice or even healing, since both her reputation for holiness and miracles, and her knowledge in the areas of the natural and medical sciences, were by then widely known.

One episode serves to demonstrate the boldness of this saint. The year of 1178, two years before her death, was characterised by a dispute with the prelates of Mainz. The archbishop, Christian, had been called temporarily to Rome. The abbess had permitted a formerly excommunicated nobleman, who had been fully reconciled with the Church and received the last sacraments, to be buried in the territory of Rupertsberg. The prelates of Mainz had asked that he be buried elsewhere. When Hildegard refused, the whole monastery was put under ecclesiastical interdict. The celebration of Mass in the monastery chapel was prohibited, the nuns were allowed to receive the Eucharist only once a month, and they had to recite the office quietly and behind closed doors. Hildegard was forced to send a letter of appeal to Archbishop Christian, who, after pondering all of the facets of the difficult question, agreed with the abbess and freed the monastery from the interdict that had disturbed the lives of the nuns for several months.

At the age of eighty-two, Hildegard became ill in the summer of 1179 and passed away, surrounded by her fellow sisters and with the reputation of holiness, at the monastery of Rupertsberg near Bingen on 17th September 1179. According to the *Vita Sanctae Hildegardis*, she had foreseen the day and time of her death long beforehand.

Attempts at Canonisation

Considered a saint already during her lifetime, and even more so immediately after her death, in part because of the miracles that took place at her intercession, Hildegard of Bingen and her cause could have followed a procedure that at the time - under the system of canonisation by the bishop was completely normal, and allowed the local ordinary or diocesan synod to proceed with canonisation through *elevatio* and *translatio*.

Following, however, a procedure that was gradually beginning to impose itself and to become ever more exclusive - founded upon the conviction of greater authoritativeness attributed to pontifical canonisation[5] - the nuns of Rupertsberg decided to approach, perhaps in 1227, Pope Gregory IX (1227-1241). Pontifical intervention was made concrete on 27th January 1228 with an apostolic letter addressed to some of the prelates of Mainz - the provost of the cathedral, Gerbodo, the dean, Walther, and the chancellor, Arnold. In the letter, Gregory IX - who among other things had been the pontifical legate in Germany from 1207-1208 and had heard about the holiness of Hildegard of Bingen - informed the aforementioned prelates of the explicit request of the Benedictines of

Bingen, entrusting to them the task of documenting the life, activity, reputation, merits and miracles of the abbess, through trustworthy testimonies.

It took the three prelates about five years to complete their task. They sent their procedural findings to Rome on 16th December 1233, through Bruno of Strasbourg, who, in obedience to the contents of the same pontifical letter, also delivered a biography of Hildegard (in all probability the *Vita Sanctae Hildegardis* by Theodoric of Echternach) and a copy of Hildegard's writings, together with an evaluation of their merit by the theology faculty of the Sorbonne in Paris, summarised by Professor William of Auxerre in the statement that "the writings of Hildegard do not contain human words, but divine words."

In spite of the absence of an official procedural conclusion, the general recognition of the holiness of Hildegard of Bingen was evident. Many authors of the thirteenth and fourteenth centuries, when they speak of the Rhenish mystic and abbess, always add to her name the title of 'Saint' in expressions such as "*sancta Hildegardis,*" "*sancta virgo Hildegardis,*" "*sancta Hildegardis prophetissa*" and "*sancta virgo Spiritus Sancti plena*". Her reputation of holiness was constantly spreading, and her name was quickly added to local martyrologies. Certain forms of devotion sprang up right away, which were duly authorised by the diocesan authorities of Mainz, who among other things granted various privileges and indulgences to the monastery of Rupertsberg. Evidence of this includes the *Octo lectiones in festo sanctae Hildegardis legendae*, composed between 1182 and 1187, and immediately incorporated into the divine office recited in her honour.

Great devotion was also reserved for Hildegard's relics. For the dedication of an altar in 1287 in the church of Saint Quirinus in Trier, for example, the relics embedded in it also included some of Hildegard's hair and part of her veil. In any case, devotion to the relics of the Rhenish abbess is attested to in the history of the following centuries as well.

In 1489 the archbishop of Mainz, Bertold of Henneberg, authorised the exhumation of Hildegard's body, following the canonical criteria and forms of the *elevatio*. This act, which from the fifth to the thirteenth century had constituted canonisation by the bishop, no longer did so in the fifteenth century.

Two centuries later, in 1660, Hildegard's relics were venerated by two Bollandist fathers, Godfried Henschenius and Daniel Papebroch, who had visited the monastery.[6] These same Bollandists added the name of the German mystic to the *Acta Sanctorum*,[7] not failing to express their disappointment over the omission of her canonisation, evidently due to inattention on the part of the first pontifical commissioners (*"Solemnis canonizatio, quae facile fieri potuisset, si primi delegati ad causam examinandam accuratius processint, nunquam est peracta"*).[8]

In reality, based on the testimony of Johannes Trithemius, Pope John XXII (1316-1334) had tried once again to introduce a process of canonisation for Hildegard of Bingen, but this time again without any result. The same pope, however, on 5th December 1324, granted various indulgences to the monastery of Rupertsberg to be dispensed on various occasions, among which was named the date of 17th September, "*festum sanctae Hildegardis*". This is the first pontifical document - the contents of which were confirmed on 26th August 1326 - in which Hildegard of Bingen is referred to as a 'saint'.[9] Documents of protection and indults of indulgence were also granted to the monastery of Rupertsberg by other popes, such as Lucius III (1181-1185) and Clement VI (1342-1352). Afterwards there was no lack of pontifical intervention aimed at confirming or expanding the indulgences to be dispensed at the monastery of Rupertsberg. On 23rd December 1767, for example, Clement XIII granted a plenary indulgence to the faithful who, with the necessary dispositions, would visit the 'Church of St Hildegard' between the evening of 16th September and sunset on 17th September.

Exemplarity of Life

In Hildegard of Bingen there exists a great consistency between her teachings and her real life. In her there is harmony between the '*forma credendi*' and the '*forma vivendi,*' between doctrine and life. It should also be emphasised that all the virtues, as they are presented and practised by the Rhenish Benedictine abbess, are firmly anchored in biblical, liturgical and patristic roots, and are reflected and implemented in the observance of the guidelines and prescriptions of the *Regula Benedicti*.

For Hildegard, virtue is part of that one good who is God himself. In order to do good, man needs a variety of virtues, which contribute to shaping and orientating his existence towards its end, which is salvation. In the *ordo virtutum* Hildegard maintains that *timor Domini* is the root of the virtuous life and *discretio* is its fulfillment and flowering.

At the beginning of her first work, *Scivias*, Hildegard sees the fear of God as a figure covered with eyes that stands directly in front of the throne of the glorious Light, and represents humility and correct intention, zeal and constancy, vigilance and the search for the presence of God. In *timor Domini* is concentrated the monastic ideal described by the *Regula Benedicti*. In that figure full of eyes, Hildegard provides a glimpse of a relationship between the fear of God and her faculty of clairvoyance. She not only makes *timor Domini* precede the reception of the visions, but she continually indicates that this virtue constitutes the beginning of all the other virtues, bringing them to development and fulfillment.

Timor Domini is accompanied by the other virtues that are particularly important in monastic life, such as humility, obedience, chastity, together with the pillars of every believer, which are faith, hope and charity: "Faith constitutes for Hildegard the horizon, in which the human being stands at the centre of creation, accepts his existence as a creature, and can realise the task determined for him by God."[10] She insists a great deal on the integrity of the faith, above all to defend the Church from the schisms and heresies present at the time.

As situated in this context of faith, the Hildegardian conception of obedience is theologically profound. For her, "only when obedience is recognised as a power of God, present at the creation of the world, only then can one judge the moral value of this virtue: a profound union with God, on the basis of which man realises the will of the Creator in the divine creation."[11] At the same time, obedience represents a particular aspect in the imitation of the incarnate Word. And the monastery is one of the privileged places of this obedience to God the creator, in imitation of his beloved Son.

As we have said, her discourse on the virtues is at the same time theological and experiential. In her words one realises how the depth of her theological vision is accompanied by existential practice. Her thought is not drily theoretical, but profoundly wise. And it is surprising, in reading her texts, to realise how deeply rooted in an authentic biblical view of faith her reasoning on the virtues is, thousands of miles away from some modern meditations on the virtues, above all on the religious virtue of obedience, which is practically dismissed to nonexistence.

Hildegard then speaks of the excellence of humility and charity, which were at work in the Incarnation of God. They are virtues that are rooted in the mystery of the Trinity of God, of the incarnation and redemption, and are entrusted to man, the image of God, so that he may attain the divine life.

Hildegard also accentuates the virtues of *castitas* and *virginitas*, both as an ascetic exercise and as a form of imitation of the incarnation of the Word in the most pure womb of Mary. Placing the incarnation at the centre of the monastic life and its doctrine, she promotes virginity, the distinctive mark of the incarnation, as the decisive ideal for herself and for her community.

After *timor Domini* and the *ordo virtutum*, there is *discretio*, the fruit of divine action in man. Human *discretio* comes from divine *discretio*. A concrete opportunity for exercising *discretio*, as the gift of wise moderation, is seen in the determination of the proper measure given to silence and speech according to the *Regula Benedicti*: "Speaking discretely consists in the fact that in the main common consultations, the monks should express themselves '*modice ac breviter*,' and that in their fraternal coexistence they should address to one another words intended to be understood as expressions of love that may be orientated towards fraternal affection."[12] *Discretio*, meaning moderation, is applied to sleeping, to eating and to fasting. And even to prayer: a healthy moderation increases the joy of praying. Moderation, discretion and balance are the recommendations that recur most frequently in the correspondence, and this leads to the supposition that they are indirect witnesses of her discrete and temperate behaviour.

But Hildegard's virtuousness appears in her Benedictine vocation, to which she adhered with conviction and determination, living the monastic ideals to the full. As the author of the writings on her visions, as the abbess of two communities of Benedictine nuns, as a leading figure in frequent contact with the personages of her time, she became ever more known outside of the monastery as well. Everyone, her fellow sisters and outside persons, could verify the consistency between her words and her behaviour. It was this concrete virtuousness that drove

Theodoric of Echternach to compose the *Vita Sanctae Hildegardis*, precisely with the intention of making known Hildegard's exemplary and holy life.

Virtue begins at home

In this biography appears her edifying attitude in the monastery first of all, with the virtues of charity toward all, of virginity, humility, modesty, silence, patience. Hildegard burned with charity and zeal. In a particular way she practiced the virtue of humility, experienced not only in the forms and degrees of Article 7 of the *Benedictine Rule*, but also in the devout acceptance of physical weakness and suffering, which made her capable of receiving the extraordinary gifts of grace. Even before it was so on the outside, her life was devout and pleasing to God in the concealment of the monastery of Disibodenberg and then in that of Rupertsberg.

The Benedictine Guibert de Gembloux (1124-1214), in a letter to his friend Bobo, expresses his impressions of Hildegard and her nuns by saying among other things that in the monastery there was such a concentration of virtue, between the mother who embraced her daughters with such charity and the daughters who submitted to their mother with such reverence, that it was hard to tell if it was the mother who surpassed her daughters in this reciprocal zeal or the other way around. This shows how the Benedictine *norma vivendi* - love, humility, obedience, discretion - was reflected not only in the writings but above all in the life of the abbess Hildegard.

In public as well Hildegard was considered a virtuous woman. In spite of her gift of the vision of divine things, she was always seen by the priests and bishops who examined her as a simple woman - humble, obedient, charitable and supremely welcoming. She was sought out by persons in need of advice or overcome by illness, to obtain graces and miracles. Her attitude was that of encouraging her neighbour in the fear of God, in the salvation of the soul and in holiness. Even her voyages of preaching had evangelising and spiritual purposes.

Particularly deep was her faith in God, who constituted the true authority for judging her behaviour. Hildegard was so open to the presence of God that all of her actions - even those which may have seemed subject to criticism (like the foundation of her own monastery or the interdict imposed because of the unauthorised burial of a previously excommunicated but later reconciled nobleman) - were the result of her blind and innocent obedience to the divine will. The episode of the nun Richardis von Stade, who against her judgement became the abbess of the monastery of Bassum and passed away shortly after her arrival there, shows how Hildegard, while demonstrating a side of human weakness, in the end was able to find reconciling words at the news of Richardis's death.

In any case, the biographer views the holy life of Hildegard in light of the fact that she was not puffed up by praise, nor dejected in adversity, but met everything with serenity and discipline. Moreover, in everything she was guided by sound doctrine concerning the nature of man, the conflict of flesh and spirit, the example of the holy fathers. The hagiographer sees in Hildegard natural capacities and charisms so united as to lead Hildegard to heavenly felicity, through an 'ascent of the mind,' as the Revelation of John promises to the victors at the end of time. She considered herself, in fact, always *coram Deo*, coming from him and going back to him.

Hildegard's comparison of herself to a feather is the most beautiful expression of her humility. She allowed herself to be borne upwards by God, the mighty king, at his pleasure: "The feather does not fly on its own, but is carried by the wind. Just so I do not have command of human doctrine or powerful forces...but I stand firm in the help of God."[13]

The Reputation of Holiness and Miracles

Mention has already been made of the numerous and substantiated attestations of the *fama sanctitatis* enjoyed by Hildegard of Bingen and reflected in the correspondence addressed to her. Here it should be sufficient to refer to just a few of them. Tenxwind, the abbess of Andernach, although she had not spared Hildegard from some critical observations, cannot help but note "the well-known fame of her holiness, which sounds stupendous to our ears."[14] Elsewhere Hildegard is referred to as a "bright and burning lantern, a most splendid lamp," given to illumine the Church, "light to console the faithful." It is acknowledged that the fame of her holiness spread everywhere with a sweet sound and with gentle perfume. As instrument of Christ and tabernacle of the Holy Spirit, in her are admired the riches of wisdom and eloquence.

Various witnesses enumerate her many virtues: discipline, devotion, piety, charity, humility, obedience, continence, chastity, mercy, prudence and many others. Some also recall the gifts of grace and privileges granted to her by God, such as visions, prophecy, contemplation, understanding, the gift of counsel and the spirit of prayer.

After her death her reputation of holiness was always present both in popular devotion and in liturgical worship. From the first years after her passing, in fact, her feast has been celebrated in Eibingen every 17th September, augmented with a procession with the relics of 'St' Hildegard. As has already been seen, this liturgical devotion was already approved and authorised in the thirteeth century by the diocesan ordinaries of Mainz, and then in the following centuries by those of Trier, Speyer and Limburg. Since 1904, the year of the foundation of the new 'St Hildegard' monastery in Eibingen, the main initiatives and most characteristic celebrations have had their point of reference in the monastery itself.

The wonder-working activity of Hildegard of Bingen is the focus of the third book of the *Vita Sanctae Hildegardis* by Theodoric of Echternach. Here it is enough to point out that very often the miracles performed through the intercession of Hildegard of Bingen have been set in relation with her writings, in demonstration of the fact that both pursue the same ends: to strengthen faith, promote understanding of the Christian message, and open the way to mercy and salvation. Every miracle, extraordinary healing or exorcism closes with thanksgiving to God and awareness of his intervention, often putting in close conjunction the miracles worked by Jesus and narrated in the Gospel with the healings obtained following the intercession of Hildegard. The Rhenish abbess herself, on the occasion of several healings, offered a final act of praise and thanksgiving to the Lord with the words, *"Nunc autem cum laude simul dicamus: Gloria tibi, Domine."*[15]

Eminens Doctrina

In her numerous writings and in the different literary genres, Hildegard aimed exclusively at the exposition of divine revelation. Her doctrinal magisterium is essentially an *interpretatio Scripturae*. Take, for example, the *Scivias*. In the six visions contained in the first part, Hildegard contemplates creation, the fall of the angels and of Adam, the celestial hierarchy. In the seven visions of the second part, she meditates on the salvific incarnation of the Son of God and his presence in the world through the Church, the fight against the devil. In the thirteen visions of the third part, finally, she considers the coming of the kingdom of God and the Last Judgement.

Her language has the difficult task of describing the indescribable, communicated to her by the celestial visions. Without entering into the numerous theological disputes of her time and fleeing from the discursive form, Hildegard enunciates the truths of the faith, emphasising the symbolic form, the poetic image, analogy, metaphor and, at times, song. The following are a few of the themes that she addresses.

The knowledge of God

This is the first task of theology. Hildegard is aware of the possibilities and limitations of the knowledge of God on the part of man. Her visions are not situated within the context of a faith that seeks understanding, but of a faith that already understands. In spite of his *incomprehensibilitas*, God can be 'intuited' through faith. The motif of the '*Deus nec totus absconditus nec totus manifestus*' - which for Hugh of St Victor constitutes the character of the human understanding of God - permeates all of Hildegard's writings. Although it shows itself in the revelation of the Old and New Testament, the mystery of God maintains at the same time a dimension of *ostensio* and *protectio*.

Creation, when viewed through faith, constitutes a first symbolic knowledge of God. Without faith, with the eye of the flesh alone, one obtains a *scientia mala*; with faith, however, a *scientia bona*. In her visions Hildegard never passes beyond the boundaries of God's unknowability, limiting her understanding and communication of the mysteries to what has already been revealed, which for this reason is accessible to every believing human being.

As for the Trinitarian mystery, Hildegard follows the optimistic Augustinian view, according to which human *ratio*, on the basis of its own self-reflection, is able to arrive at an image of trinity and to deduce from this the divine Trinity. A century later, St Thomas Aquinas would explain that the knowledge of the Trinity *nullo modo potest demonstrative probari*.[16]

Hildegard instead maintains that the *mysterium Trinitatis* can be contemplated and understood. In the seventh vision of the third part of *Scivias*, she writes:

> "The holy and ineffable Trinity in its supreme unity was hidden from the servants of the ancient law. But in the new grace it was revealed to those freed from servitude. The faithful must now believe with a simple and humble heart in the one God in three Persons, without seeking to subject this to imprudent investigations....This column that you see at the western corner of the aforementioned edifice is a symbolic form of the true Trinity....The column is placed on the west because the Son of God became incarnate when the sunset of time was drawing near. He glorified his Father everywhere, and promised to the disciples the Holy Spirit. The Son himself, fulfilling the will of the Father, went to meet death and became a good example to men, so that they as well may live in the edifice of the supreme Father and perform true good works in the Holy Spirit."[17]

The Trinitarian self-communication of God has its historical place in the death of the Son on the cross, which brings the *vera fides* to believers.

The conception of man

Hildegard begins with the biblical account of the creation of man in the image and likeness of God (cf. *Gn* 1:26). She sees the divine image of man in his rationality, made up of intellect and will. The intellect can distinguish good from evil and perform the function of *magister*, which allows the understanding of all things, even the divinity and humanity of God. The will drives man to perform every work, both good and evil. Hildegard's organic vision is illustrated by the metaphor of the tree: "*Intellectus* is in the soul like the sap in the branches and leaves of the tree, *voluntas* is like the flower, *animus* like the first fruit, *ratio* like the fruit come to perfect maturity, and *sensus* like the height and extension of its fullness."[18]

Man is seen as a unity of body and soul, with a positive appreciation of bodily nature. Rather than the pessimistic Platonic vision, the early medieval authors are closer to the metaphysical Aristotelian vision, which would then spread in the thirteenth century. The weak and fragile body must protect man from pride and arrogance, and constantly remind him of his identity as a creature. Moreover, through the body itself man gains greater merit. The fact that the body was not granted to man as a useless burden to be disposed of is demonstrated by the vision of Hildegard in which she sees the souls of the saints who are eagerly awaiting reunion with their mortal bodies. As for the resurrection of Christ, so also for the human body eschatological fulfillment means a transformation and resurrection unto eternal life.

To the relationship between man and woman Hildegard adds reflections on temptation, original sin, sexual desire and death. Reaffirming the substantial creatural equality between man and woman, for her the creation of Eve from the rib of Adam refers to the fact that woman was given to man as a partner: "*in consortium dilectionis*," "*socia*." She then emphasises the multiple aspects of the mutual correlation between man and woman: "Woman permits man to see himself in her like his mirror image, and therefore to recognise woman as made in his image and likeness, and at the same time he sees in her his future children."[19] Unlike the other authors of the time, who saw in original sin the extreme frailty of woman, for Hildegard it was the ardent love of Adam for Eve that gave the devil the opportunity to tempt Eve first. So instead of confirming the current doctrinal opinion of the punishment of man with concupiscence after his transgression, Hildegard turns her attention to the punishment of Eve with pain, from which emerges mercy.

As for human existence, one of the most powerful images of Christianity presents existence as a reality on a journey, and its fulfilment as a homecoming. For Hildegard as well, man is *viator*. Earthly existence is a combat, a *militia*. Man always finds himself at a crossroads: he can do good and avoid evil, thus manifesting his *rationalitas*.

It is here that Hildegard establishes her doctrine on virtue, presented in a Christological vein. It is the Son of God made man who is the subject of all the virtues, as of every virtuous life. It is Christ who is the cause of every virtue, such that the *imitatio Christi* means living a virtuous existence in Christ. Hildegard often calls virtue *scientia Dei, gratia Dei, sapientia Dei*. A holy life has its origin in the charity of the Holy Spirit, who pours into hearts the good fragrance of the virtues.

In Hildegard's doctrine of the virtues there is an original theological fabric of great relevance in avoiding the sociopsychological leveling to which the virtues are subjected. For the Rhenish abbess, virtuousness is the aim of human existence. The holy light of God is refracted in the virtuous conduct of man in many concrete forms, such as love, mercy, patience, humility, obedience. Through his virtuous effort man experiences his Christiform perfection.

The Sacraments

For Hildegard, the Sacraments are places of salvation. The first Sacrament is the Church, which God has used to communicate and share his salvation with believers through its seven Sacraments. In the language of her day 'the Sacrament' with no further specification referred to the Eucharist. Its attention was directed mainly to the relative metaphysical questions, above all to the divine action which, through the mediation of the priesthood, changes the gifts placed on the altar into the Body and Blood of Christ. The efficacy of the Sacrament is manifested in the sanctification of believers, in purification from sin, in the grace of redemption, in charity and in all of the highest virtues. For Hildegard, the Eucharist, rather than being investigated, must be welcomed with faith for the sake of its benefits. Thus the only suitable attitude is that of veneration and adoration.

The cosmos

The cosmology of Hildegard is completely biblical and constitutes the central message of her writings: "the world created by God, at the centre of which man recognises himself as loved by the Creator, is the genuine space-time of the encounter between the Creator and his image."[20]

As a microcosm, man is not only at the centre of creation, but also contains within his body all of the elements of the world. From all eternity God has contemplated in man the entirety of creation. Therefore only man can know, see, feel and experience God.

God, in fact, allows himself to be seen (*videtur*). Man cannot have a direct vision of God. His temporal seeing is a seeing as in a mirror (cf. *1 Co* 13:12). Faith, as an interior eye, is the most powerful means for knowing God.

God also allows himself to be known (*cognoscitur*), above all through creation. There is also a second domain of the knowledge of God, and that is fidelity to his word contained in the Old and New Testament. In this knowledge, man's bodily nature, rather than being an obstacle, is an opportunity for further knowledge. The definitive vision of God cannot be obtained without the body, because with the Incarnation the Son of God belongs to humanity.

God allows himself to be heard (*auditur*). In the structure and in the course of the visions, *auditus* plays just as important a role as *visio*. And hearing involves not only speech, but also song. In order to be perceived, the word must be heard, it must resound. The sound of the word of God creates life and is manifested in creatures. Through the creative word, even those creatures which are not marked by *rationalitas* experience its reverberation. Man responds to the voice of God through his *rationalitas*, which manifests itself in two ways: *in voce oris*, through the liturgical celebration and the divine service, conducted with words, music and singing; and *in voce cordis*, which is expressed in the virtuous life of men, and of the saints in particular.[21] Because of this Hildegard frequently interprets human existence as a harmony and a symphony: "while harmony signifies the restoration of creation and the full experience of redemption, the present human existence with its dangers, contradiction and sins corresponds to a symphony, to a combination of sounds and chords at the same time harmonious and dissonant. In this symphony God makes heard above all his mercy."[22]

God, finally, allows himself to be experienced (*experitur*). He lets himself be known not only in the cognitive dimension, but in a holistic way: all of the senses of man play an important role in guiding men to a complete experience of God.

Sacra Doctrina

Hildegard's teaching is aimed at guiding man on the path of salvation. Significant in this regard is the title of her first work, *Scivias*. With respect to the current version, which translates the title as *You know the ways*, the title *Scivias*, which is a *hapax legomenon* of the whole of Latin literature, is a substantive form that can be rendered in English as 'road marker' or 'indicator of the path.' In this way, the title of the work itself expresses the character of the whole *eximia et eminens doctrina* of Hildegard of Bingen: "Assimilating her work today means reformulating and bringing up to date these road markers."[23]

In all of her work, Hildegard wants to manifest God the creator in all the breadth of his love.

Love for humanity. God loves man, his most splendid work, to whom he gives the glory, honour and beauty lost by the fallen angels. Humanity is the tenth angelic choir. The love of God is offered not only to the innocent man of creation, but above all to fallen man, toward whom his mercy and unconditional love are directed.

Love for the cosmos. God loves the world, which he brought from nothing out of love, and therefore the divine charity abounds in all creatures, from the lowest on the cosmological scale to the highest. Since the world is a divine epiphany, in understanding it man cannot separate it from the creator. In separating it one obtains only myopic information about nature. Moreover, with an arrogant and overweening exploration of nature man could commit abuses both with regard to creation and with regard to his own ethical and cognitive capacities.

Love for God. The Church, for Hildegard, bears within itself the two primary Sacraments: the Trinity and the Incarnation. And it is therefore in the Church that God manifests his intra-divine love, the Trinitarian mystery. From God's love for himself, from the mysterious mutual relationship of the divine Persons comes the knowledge of the mystery of God which is love. Christ, with his divine beauty, is the revealer of the charity of God:

> "The beautiful figure of Christ is not only directed toward men from the primordial foundations of the Trinity, but is directed by men toward God. Christ is the great mediator; as the divine Son of God he is love in himself, and in his sacred humanity he

represents at the same time the love of man for God. On the basis of his earthly existence he is able to represent the whole of humanity before God."[24]

Love for the Church. God loves the Church, bride and mother. The exceptional beauty of the Church as bride, which Hildegard praises in her songs with a language difficult to surpass, consists in the fact that she is at the same time virgin and mother. This puts the Church in close connection with Mary. The Church is the *constructio viventium animarum*. Although the ancient Church was born and lived in justice, over time the individual faithful often have not been faithful witnesses of their baptism. Hildegard denounces certain deplorable situations: each individual Christian wants to be his own legislator; those who should have a teacher instead want to teach and direct themselves. As a result non-Christians, being unable to rely on the witness of Christians, cannot know and obtain the salvation of their lives.

The Perennial Validity of Hildegard

In conclusion, the doctrine of Hildegard is distinguished by a few precise characteristics which make it *eminent* both for the profundity and correctness of its interpretations, firmly anchored in the biblical texts, and for the originality of its visions, which surpass the limited historical context of their time, projecting themselves over the centuries with a particular efficacy and luminosity.

The writings of Hildegard, touched by a special grace of 'intellectual charity,' manifest a particular theological freshness and authenticity in the contemplation and narration of the mystery of the Most Holy Trinity, the Incarnation, the Church, humanity. Her doctrine is a true *summa theologica*, springing from her spiritual understanding of things and from her heart on fire with the love of God the Trinity.

But in the author's view, the summit of her magisterium resides in the heartrending appeal for a virtuous life, inside and outside of the monastery. Hildegard's understanding of the consecrated life, for example, is a lesson in authentic 'theological metaphysics,' because it is firmly rooted in the theological virtue of faith as the only plausible attitude for complete dedication to religious obedience, chastity and poverty.

The Benedictine vision of obedience, which incorporates within itself all of the religious virtues and leads to the peak of perfection, constitutes for Hildegard the only horizon of a successful religious existence, seen as participation in Christ's obedience to the Father. In this, the people of today must perceive the prophetic voice of Hildegard as an invitation to recover the essentials of consecrated life, trimming it of spurious and mistaken interpretations.

The influence of Hildegard's writings

The doctrine of Hildegard has constituted a point of reference in very critical periods of the history of the Church, for example in the conflict with the mendicant orders between the thirteenth and fourteenth centuries, and in particular during the Protestant Reformation of the sixteenth century. A detailed knowledge of Hildegard's works came about with the spread of the printing press. The first printed work, the *Scivias*, saw the light of day in 1513. In the following centuries all of her works were published, and now the complete writings are available in critical editions.

The rich and complex literary production of Hildegard of Bingen finds its internal centrality in the fact that it is understood as an interpretation of the incarnate Logos in the context of the twelfth century. Hildegard does not address the controversial questions of her time according to monastic or scholastic exegesis, but begins with Christ himself, the *'forma credendi,'* as the fundamental cause of her writing. *'Forma credendi'* and *'forma vivendi'* are intimately connected for Hildegard.

At the basis of her life is the rule of Saint Benedict, the monastic liturgy and the internalisation of Sacred Scripture as the norm of Christian life. From these three parameters springs also the *'forma credendi,'* which is nourished with the interpretation of Scripture and finds its central point in the Incarnation. The immediate reflection takes place in the *'conversatio morum,'* which delineates and actualises in the life of every man a historical-salvific process orientated towards conversion and to the realisation of the *opus Dei* through the *virtutes*. On the basis of such elements one can also verify a profound internal unity that permeates all of Hildegard's writings.

At the basis of Hildegard's works is the teaching of the Apostles and the knowledge of patristic literature, but also of the writings of authors of her own time. Hildegard's prophetic mission starts from the description and interpretation of the visions, and culminates in the transmission of the proclamation of the Incarnation - of the Word of God who proceeds from the Father, becomes incarnate in Christ and must be proclaimed to humanity. In this prophetic mission "Hildegard sees herself and her nuns in the imitation of Christ according to the model of the Virgin who becomes pregnant,"[25] ready to give birth to the Word who is Christ himself, for the salvation of the world.

Relevance

The relevance of Hildegard's works has been emphasised repeatedly in recent decades. For example, in the 1940 *Rescritto* of the Sacred Congregation of Rites, it is clearly affirmed that Hildegard can be seen as a star that shines with such a splendid light as to justify the great veneration attributed to her in past centuries, and also in our time. The saint, in fact, promoted the religious life and the correction of customs by travelling tirelessly across Germany. Moreover, she wrote a great deal on both mystical theology and the natural sciences, so much so as to be able to be considered today as the patroness of all those Catholic women who pursue higher studies.

The 1979 Petition to the Pope from the German bishops also emphasised some of the aspects of Hildegard's relevance:

1. her charismatic and speculative capacity, which can give spiritual encouragement to contemporary theology;

2. Hildegard is a model and encouragement for the scholarly and pastoral efforts of the many women academically trained in theology;

3. the understanding of nature as the creation of God, very much present in Hildegard's writings, is of particular interest today;

4. recognising her as a Doctor of the Church would give a powerful impulse to the female ideal of consecration;

5. finally, her musical work could also have a certain influence on today's Church music.

Also in 1979, Blessed John Paul II, writing to Cardinal Hermann Volk, the Bishop of Mainz, at the eight hundredth anniversary of her death, said about Hildegard:

"Endowed from a young age with special and advanced gifts, St Hildegard penetrated the mysteries of theology, medicine, music and the other arts, left numerous writings on these arts, and brought to light the relationship between redemption and creation. She loved the Church in a singular way: burning with this love she did not hesitate to leave the monastery as an intrepid promoter of truth and peace in order to meet with the bishops, the civil authorities, and the Emperor himself, and did not hesitate to dialogue with multitudes of men. She who, always infirm in her physical health but rather vigorous in spiritual power and truly a 'strong woman,' once called the 'prophetess of Germany,' at this anniversary seems to address with passion the Christians and non-Christians of her people. The very life and action of this illustrious saint teach that union with God and the fulfillment of the divine will are goods greatly to be desired, above all for those who have chosen the path of the religious vocation: precisely to these latter I would like to address the words of St Hildegard: 'Look and walk upon the right path' (S. Hildegard, Epist. CXL: PL 197, 371). Christians will feel encouraged to translate in the practice of life the evangelical proclamation in our age. Moreover this teacher, filled with the presence of God, clearly indicates that the world can be ruled and administered with justice only if it is considered as the creation of the loving and provident Father who is in heaven. Finally, with the solicitude that characterised her work as a tireless minister of the Saviour with regard to the spiritual and material needs of her contemporaries, she will lead the men of good will of our time to help their brothers and sisters who find themselves in difficulty."

The Holy Father Benedict XVI also emphasised the relevance of Hildegard's holiness and doctrine in two catecheses of September 2010. In both of them Hildegard is always referred to as 'saint.' In the first she is called "a woman of culture and of lofty spirituality, capable of dealing competently with the organisational aspects of cloistered life," while "her manner of exercising the ministry of authority is an example for every religious community." He emphasises "Hildegard's spiritual prestige," which earned her the honorific title of "Teutonic prophetess."

In the second catechesis, Benedict XVI presents the spiritual, theological, and doctrinal content of the life and writings of 'St' Hildegard in such a clear and evocative way that they alone would suffice to motivate and justify the naming of the Rhenish Benedictine abbess as "Doctor of the Church." In fact, the Pope says, she "was distinguished for her spiritual wisdom and the holiness of her life." He emphasises her mystical visions, which "refer to the principal events of salvation history, and use a language for the most part poetic and symbolic." And again: "With the characteristic traits of feminine sensitivity, Hildegard develops at the very heart of her work the theme of the mysterious marriage between God and humanity that is brought about in the Incarnation. On the tree of the Cross take place the nuptials of the Son of God with the Church, his Bride, filled with grace and the ability to give new children to God, in the love of the Holy Spirit." And finally, "Hildegard stresses the deep relationship that exists between man and God and reminds us that the whole creation, of which man is the summit, receives life from the Trinity."

He also emphasises Hildegard's artistic versatility, her musical compositions, her writings on medicine and the natural sciences, and also the popularity that she enjoyed, easily seen in the rich epistolary correspondence, among other things. He also emphasises her action in defence of the Roman See against the powerful interference of Emperor Frederick I and her pastoral voyages in defence of the Faith and against the abuses of the clergy, with the promotion everywhere of "a sincere spirit of repentance and a demanding process of conversion."

Finally, the current abbess of Eibingen, in a letter addressed to the Holy Father in December 2010, also shows the 'modernity' of Hildegard, a woman capable of speaking to the minds and hearts of the men of our time, above all to those far from the Church and from the Faith. She highlights her great and impassioned love for the Church and for its authority, together with a strong conviction of the dignity and sacredness of religious and priestly life. The abbess concludes with the request that the "prophetess of Germany" be attributed the title of "Doctor of the Church," something that should be considered in every way a sign of the times in our day.

Message of Holiness

But the perennial relevance of Hildegard of Bingen resides above all in her holiness, which is never eclipsed. Together with the heroic exercise of the baptismal virtues she united an extraordinary capacity for looking upward, toward the mystery of God the Trinity and of the Incarnation, to guide and illuminate her own personal history and that of her time.

Hildegard speaks of God, prays to God, stands in the presence of God. Sacred Scripture is the spring of her *sacra doctrina*. Hildegard loves the Church, spends herself for it in counsel, in preaching, in admonition, but above all in her personal sanctification. She is a woman who lives her life of consecration as a spiritual talent to bear fruit a hundredfold not only in prayer, but also in action, such that consecration may also become ecclesiastical service.

It therefore seems justified to confer the title of Doctor of the Church on this nun who with her eminent doctrine has contributed to the deepening of the knowledge of Divine Revelation, enriching the theological patrimony of the Church and procuring for the faithful means for growing in faith and charity. *Scivias*, her masterpiece, is nothing other than an inspired handbook for following the way of God, which is the way of truth, of goodness, of justice, and of peace.[26]

Benedict XVI and Hildegard of Bingen

The following are the two papal catecheses dedicated to Hildegard of Bingen, on 1st and 8th September 2010.

Catechesis of Benedict XVI at the General Audience (Castelgandolfo) of 1st September 2010.[27]

"Dear Brothers and Sisters,

In 1988, on the occasion of the Marian Year, Venerable John Paul II wrote an Apostolic Letter entitled *Mulieris Dignitatem* on the precious role that women have played and play in the life of the Church. 'The Church', one reads in it, 'gives thanks for all the manifestations of the feminine "genius" which have appeared in the course of history, in the midst of all peoples and nations; she gives thanks for all the charisms that the Holy Spirit distributes to women in the history of the People of God, for all the victories which she owes to their faith, hope and charity: she gives thanks for all the fruits of feminine holiness' (n. 31).

"Various female figures stand out for the holiness of their lives and the wealth of their teaching even in those centuries of history that we usually call the

Middle Ages. Today I would like to begin to present one of them to you: St Hildegard of Bingen, who lived in Germany in the twelfth century. She was born in 1098, probably at Bermersheim, Rhineland, not far from Alzey, and died in 1179 at the age of 81, in spite of having always been in poor health. Hildegard belonged to a large noble family and her parents dedicated her to God from birth for his service. At the age of eight she was offered for the religious state (in accordance with the Rule of St Benedict, Chapter 59), and, to ensure that she received an appropriate human and Christian formation, she was entrusted to the care of the consecrated widow Uda of Gölklheim and then to Jutta of Spanheim who had taken the veil at the Benedictine Monastery of St Disibodenberg. A small cloistered women's monastery was developing there that followed the Rule of St Benedict. Hildegard was clothed by Bishop Otto of Bamberg and in 1136, upon the death of Mother Jutta who had become the community *magistra* (prioress), the sisters chose Hildegard to succeed her. She fulfilled this office making the most of her gifts as a woman of culture and of lofty spirituality, capable of dealing competently with the organisational aspects of cloistered life. A few years later, partly because of the increasing number of young women who were knocking at the monastery door, Hildegard broke away from the dominating male monastery of St Disibodenburg with her community, taking it to Bingen, calling it after St Rupert and here she spent the rest of her days. Her manner of exercising the ministry of authority is an example for every religious community: she inspired holy emulation in the practice of good to such an extent that, as time was to tell, both the mother and her daughters competed in mutual esteem and in serving each other.

"During the years when she was superior of the Monastery of St Disibodenberg, Hildegard began to dictate the mystical visions that she had been receiving for some time to the monk Volmar, her spiritual director, and to Richardis von Stade, her secretary, a sister of whom she was very fond. As always happens in the life of true mystics, Hildegard too wanted to put herself under the authority of wise people to discern the origin of her visions, fearing that they were the product of illusions and did not come from God. She thus turned to a person who was most highly esteemed in the Church in those times: St Bernard of Clairvaux, of whom I have already spoken in several catecheses. He calmed and encouraged Hildegard. However, in 1147 she received a further, very important approval. Pope Eugene III, who was presiding at a Synod in Trier, read a text dictated by

Hildegard presented to him by Archbishop Henry of Mainz. The Pope authorised the mystic to write down her visions and to speak in public. From that moment Hildegard's spiritual prestige continued to grow so that her contemporaries called her the 'Teutonic prophetess'. This, dear friends, is the seal of an authentic experience of the Holy Spirit, the source of every charism: the person endowed with supernatural gifts never boasts of them, never flaunts them and, above all, shows complete obedience to the ecclesial authority. Every gift bestowed by the Holy Spirit, is in fact intended for the edification of the Church and the Church, through her pastors, recognises its authenticity.

"I shall speak again next Wednesday about this great woman, this 'prophetess' who also speaks with great timeliness to us today, with her courageous ability to discern the signs of the times, her love for creation, her medicine, her poetry, her music, which today has been reconstructed, her love for Christ and for his Church which was suffering in that period too, wounded also in that time by the sins of both priests and lay people, and far better loved as the Body of Christ. Thus St Hildegard speaks to us; we shall speak of her again next Wednesday. Thank you for your attention."

Catechesis of Benedict XVI at the General Audience (Paul VI Audience Hall) of 8th September 2010.[28]

"Dear Brothers and Sisters,

Today I would like to take up and continue my Reflection on St Hildegard of Bingen, an important female figure of the Middle Ages who was distinguished for her spiritual wisdom and the holiness of her life. Hildegard's mystical visions resemble those of the Old Testament prophets: expressing herself in the cultural and religious categories of her time, she interpreted the Sacred Scriptures in the light of God, applying them to the various circumstances of life. Thus all those who heard her felt the need to live a consistent and committed Christian lifestyle. In a letter to St Bernard the mystic from the Rhineland confesses: 'The vision fascinates my whole being: I do not see with the eyes of the body but it appears to me in the spirit of the mysteries....I recognise the deep meaning of what is expounded on in the Psalter, in the Gospels and in other books, which have been shown to me in the vision. This vision burns like a flame in my breast and in my soul and teaches me to understand the text profoundly' (*Epistolarium pars prima* I-XC: CCCM 91).

"Hildegard's mystical visions have a rich theological content. They refer to the principal events of salvation history, and use a language for the most part poetic and symbolic. For example, in her best known work entitled *Scivias*, that is, 'You know the ways' she sums up in thirty five visions the events of the history of salvation from the creation of the world to the end of time. With the characteristic traits of feminine sensitivity, Hildegard develops at the very heart of her work the theme of the mysterious marriage between God and humanity that is brought about in the Incarnation. On the tree of the Cross take place the nuptials of the Son of God with the Church, his Bride, filled with grace and the ability to give new children to God, in the love of the Holy Spirit (cf. *Visio tertia*: PL 197, 453c).

"From these brief references we already see that theology too can receive a special contribution from women because they are able to talk about God and the mysteries of faith using their own particular intelligence and sensitivity. I therefore encourage all those who carry out this service to do it with a profound ecclesiastical spirit, nourishing their own reflection with prayer and looking to the great riches, not yet fully explored, of the medieval mystic tradition, especially that represented by luminous models such as Hildegard of Bingen.

"The Rhenish mystic is also the author of other writings, two of which are particularly important since, like *Scivias*, they record her mystical visions: they are the *Liber Vitae Meritorum* (Book of the Merits of Life) and the *Liber Divinorum Operum* (Book of the Divine Works), also called *De Operatione Dei*. In the former she describes a unique and powerful vision of God who gives life to the cosmos with his power and his light. Hildegard stresses the deep relationship that exists between man and God and reminds us that the whole of creation, of which man is the summit, receives life from the Trinity. The work is centred on the relationship between virtue and vice, which is why human beings must face the daily challenge of vice that distances them on their way towards God and of virtue that benefits them. The invitation is to distance themselves from evil in order to glorify God and, after a virtuous existence, enter the life that consists 'wholly of joy'. In her second work that many consider her masterpiece she once again describes creation in its relationship with God and the centrality of the human being, expressing a strong Christo-centrism with a biblical-Patristic flavour. The saint, who presents five visions inspired by the Prologue of the Gospel according to St John, cites the words of the Son to the Father: "The whole task that you wanted and entrusted to me

I have carried out successfully, and so here I am in you and you in me and we are one" (Pars III, *Visio X*: PL 197, 1025a).

"Finally, in other writings Hildegard manifests the versatility of interests and cultural vivacity of the female monasteries of the Middle Ages, in a manner contrary to the prejudices which still weighed on that period. Hildegard took an interest in medicine and in the natural sciences as well as in music, since she was endowed with artistic talent. Thus she composed hymns, antiphons and songs, gathered under the title: *Symphonia Harmoniae Caelestium Revelationum* (Symphony of the Harmony of Heavenly Revelations), that were performed joyously in her monasteries, spreading an atmosphere of tranquillity and that have also come down to us. For her, the entire creation is a symphony of the Holy Spirit who is in himself joy and jubilation.

"The popularity that surrounded Hildegard impelled many people to seek her advice. It is for this reason that we have so many of her letters at our disposal. Many male and female monastic communities turned to her, as well as bishops and abbots. And many of her answers still apply for us. For instance, Hildegard wrote these words to a community of women religious: 'The spiritual life must be tended with great dedication. At first the effort is burdensome because it demands the renunciation of caprices of the pleasures of the flesh and of other such things. But if she lets herself be enthralled by holiness a holy soul will find even contempt for the world sweet and lovable. All that is needed is to take care that the soul does not shrivel'[29]. And when the Emperor Frederic Barbarossa caused a schism in the Church by supporting at least three anti-popes against Alexander III, the legitimate Pope, Hildegard did not hesitate, inspired by her visions, to remind him that even he, the Emperor, was subject to God's judgement. With fearlessness, a feature of every prophet, she wrote to the Emperor these words as spoken by God: 'You will be sorry for this wicked conduct of the godless who despise me! Listen, O King, if you wish to live! Otherwise my sword will pierce you!' (ibid., p. 412).

"With the spiritual authority with which she was endowed, in the last years of her life Hildegard set out on journeys, despite her advanced age and the uncomfortable conditions of travel, in order to speak to the people of God. They all listened willingly, even when she spoke severely: they considered her a messenger sent by God. She called above all the monastic communities and the clergy to a life in conformity with their vocation. In a special way Hildegard countered the movement of German *cátari* (Cathars). They (*cátari* means literally 'pure') advocated a radical reform of the Church, especially to combat the abuses of the clergy. She harshly reprimanded them for seeking to subvert the very nature of the Church, reminding them that a true renewal of the ecclesial community is obtained with a sincere spirit of repentance and a demanding process of conversion, rather than with a change of structures. This is a message that we should never forget. Let us always invoke the Holy Spirit, so that he may inspire in the Church holy and courageous women, like St Hildegard of Bingen, who, developing the gifts they have received from God, make their own special and valuable contribution to the spiritual development of our communities and of the Church in our time."

Endnotes

[1] John Paul II, Letter to Hermann Volk, Bishop of Mainz, on the occasion of the 800th anniversary of the death of St Hildegard (8th September 1979).
[2] Benedict XVI, General Audience of 1st September 2010.
[3] The entirety of chapter XLI of Book 1 is dedicated to the canonisation equivalent: c.f. Benedict XIV (Prospero Lambertini), *De Servorum Dei Beatificatione et Beatorum Canonizatione*, vol. I/2, (Città del Vaticano, 2011), pp. 9-88.
[4] Ibid, pp. 9-10.
[5] Cf. Congregation for the Causes of Saints, *Le Cause dei Santi*, (Libreria Editrice Vaticana, 2012), p. 156.
[6] *Acta Sanctorum*, Maii III, p. 502.
[7] *Acta Sanctorum*, Septembris V, pp. 629-690.
[8] Patrologia Latina 197, p. 89.
[9] The original of the pontifical document is kept in the Staatsarchiv of Koblenz, Grosses Privilegienbuch vom Rupertsberg, Abt. 701, A IV, nr. 3, f. 161r.
[10] Rainer Bernd and Maura Zátonyi, *Informatio super virtutibus, fama sanctitatis e miraculorum Hildegardis Birgensis, in Congregatio de Causis Sanctorum, Positio super Canonizatione et Ecclesiae Doctoratu Hildegardis Birgensis*, (Rome, 2012), p. 86.
[11] Ibid, p. 87.
[12] Ibid, p. 92.
[13] Ibid. p. 105.
[14] Michael Embach, *Profilo biografico e produzione letteraria di Ildegarda di Bingen, in Congregatio de causis sanctorum, Positio*, p. 52.
[15] *Hildegardis Bingensis, Epistolarium*, Pars 2: XCI-CCLr, edited by L. Van Acker, (Turnhout, 1993), n. 158r, p. 353, 33.
[16] Thomas Aquinas, *Expositio super librum Boethii De Trinitate*, q. 1, a. 4.
[17] Hildegard of Bingen, *Scivias* (ed. Giovanna della Croce), (Città del Vaticano, Libreria Editrice Vaticana, 2002), pp 219-220. The booklet contains only a few selections from the work.
[18] Rainer Bernd, Maura Zátonyi, *Ildegarda di Bingen e la sua "esimia et eminens doctrina," in Congregatio de Causis Sanctorum, Positio*, pp. 369-370.
[19] Ibid, p. 373.
[20] Ibid, p. 403.

[21] Ibid, p. 421.
[22] Ibid, pp. 421-422.
[23] Ibid, p. 425.
[24] Ibid, p. 450.
[25] Rainer Bernd, Maura Zátonyi, *Gli scritti di Ildegarda di Bingen, in Congregatio de Causis Sanctorum, Positio*, p. 280.
[26] On 7th October 2012, Benedict XVI proclaimed St Hildegard of Bingen a Doctor of the Usniversal Church.
[27] For the text, see *L'Osservatore Romano*, 2nd September 2010, 8.
[28] For the text, see *L'Osservatore Romano*, 9th September 2010, 8.
[29] E. Gronau, Hildegard. *Vita di una donna profetica alle origini dell'età moderna*, (Milan, 1996), p. 402.